BOB FOSSE

Jenai Cutcher

rosen
central™

The Rosen Publishing Group, Inc., New York

Thanks to my teachers

Published in 2006 by The Rosen Publishing Group, Inc.
29 East 21st Street, New York, NY 10010

Library of Congress Cataloging-in-Publication Data

Cutcher, Jenai.
Bob Fosse / Jenai Cutcher.— 1st ed.
      p. cm. — (The library of American choreographers)
Includes bibliographical references and index.
ISBN 1-4042-0446-6 (lib. bdg.)
ISBN 1-4042-0640-X (pbk. bdg.)
1. Fosse, Bob, 1927-1987. 2. Choreographers—United States—Biography.
I. Title. II. Series.
GV1785.C88C88 2006
792.8'2'092—dc22

                                                                    2005000403
Manufactured in the United States of America

On the cover: Bob Fosse in 1987. Background: The cast of the Broadway
show *Big Deal* in rehearsal with Bob Fosse (*center*) in 1985.

Contents

Introduction

In the musical *Sweet Charity*, three women express their desire to find and live a better life in the song "There's Gotta Be Something Better Than This." Unhappy with their present circumstances, each character begins to ponder what the future might hold. Each woman becomes more and more elated at all the possibilities and how she plans to get out and live this new life. Their singing expresses this, but their exciting dancing stresses this meaning even more. Perhaps the choreography expressed this idea so well because the song's words were ones the choreographer, Bob Fosse, seemed to live by. This same zest for life, this eagerness to "get out and live it," drove Bob Fosse through a full and successful career as one of America's best choreographers.

The Early Years

1

If it weren't for his older sister, Bob Fosse may have never become one of America's most famous dancers and choreographers. Robert Louis Fosse was born in Chicago, Illinois, on June 23, 1927. He was the fifth child of Cyril and Sadie Fosse. At that time, Bob had three older brothers and one sister. His younger sister, Marianne, was born ten years later.

Dancing first entered Bob's life through his family. His parents loved ballroom dancing and taught their children the foxtrot, jitterbug, and other social dances. In those days, it was not common practice for boys to attend dancing school. For that reason, Sadie Fosse's teenage sons were excused, but she insisted that her daughter Patricia take formal dance lessons. Patsy was quite shy and did not want to go to dance class alone, so Bobby, being the youngest at the time, was forced to accompany her. This small turn of events was

Bob is pictured here at an early stage of his career, emulating his role models, Gene Kelly and Fred Astaire. His childhood vaudeville days as Bob Riff would follow him throughout his professional career. The formal tuxedo and dancing cane are typical of vaudeville dance attire for men.

all that was needed to set the wheels in motion for eight-year-old Bobby's future career in dance.

Life as a Riff Brother

Bobby and Patsy attended the Chicago Academy for Theatre Arts, a small studio run by Frederic (Fred) Weaver. Marguerite Comerford was the Fosse children's teacher. Bobby loved his dancing lessons, but two years later, he and Patsy had to quit. The Great Depression (1929–1939) had taken its toll on the United States, and the family could no longer afford such an extravagance. Patsy was probably relieved, but Bobby was doing well as a dance student and already serving as the emcee of the school's annual recital. It was then that Weaver, the artistic director and manager of vaudeville acts, struck a deal with Bobby. He could remain at the school on scholarship if he worked as one half of a new act that Weaver was developing. A portion of Bobby's earnings as a performer would go to Weaver as payment for his lessons. Bobby's father agreed to this arrangement but expressed disdain for his son's involvement with dance.

Weaver paired Bobby with a boy named Charles Grass to create a standard dance duo for vaudeville shows. The most popular dancing acts of the time were based on tap dance, singing, and acrobatics. Many of these performers were brothers, such as the Nicholas Brothers and the Berry Brothers. So Bobby and Charles became known as the Riff Brothers (Dancers Extraordinary). A "riff" is both a tap dance step and a repeated musical phrase. Although the boys were not related, they looked very much alike, so the name worked well for them.

For months the boys rehearsed with Weaver and their dance teacher, Miss Comerford. As a dancer, Bobby had to struggle to correct some of his movement habits. He was left-handed and always wanted to turn to the left.

Because Charlie was right-handed, which is more common, Bobby was forced to turn to the right. Also, Miss Comerford liked to see straight arms with the palms facing down and fingers together. No matter how much she reminded him, Bobby always had his arms bent at the elbow with his palms facing out and his fingers spread wide open.

Despite these habits, Bob Fosse had a natural talent as a performer. His personality worked well with his partner's to create a solid act. After a charming opening, each boy would perform a short solo. Bob's was fast and packed with tap steps while Charles's was lighter and more graceful. They ended with a challenge sequence that involved flash choreography: each boy would take a turn at performing a short series of tricks and other steps meant to impress the audience. Once the excitement was built, they would return to dancing in unison. They would end with a big finish of kicks, turns, and trenches—straight leg kicks to the back with the opposite arm reaching down to the floor.

The Riff Brothers's first professional performance was actually in an amateur contest. They wowed the audience with their polished appearance in formal dress suits complete with coattails, and they danced well enough to win first prize.

At twelve years old, Bob Fosse's first earnings as a dancer were $4.50 and an ice-cream sundae. Charles and Bob continued to perform as the Riff Brothers all around Chicago in theaters and in small nightclubs. Even though Bob spent many hours in rehearsal and was out late performing in shows, he was always a good student and entered high school at the top of his class.

Since his father did not approve of Bob's dancing, Bob never discussed his performances with his family. Also, with his three older brothers off fighting in World War II (1939–1945), the family had other things to worry about. The Fosse household was full of women, including Bob's mother, his older and younger sisters, and the wives of his brothers. Most of the dancers Bob knew were also female, so Bob became comfortable around the opposite sex at an early age. Beginning in high school and throughout his life, he would almost always have a girlfriend. Later, female dancers would play a very important role in bringing Fosse's choreography to life.

As situations in the world and in Bob's home life developed, things changed at the dance studio, too. Miss Comerford moved away, and Weaver added Bob and Charles to the faculty. Although only Charles ever actually taught class, Bob was constantly working out new routines in the studio now that he had his own key. In the academy recital of 1943, Bob appeared with Charles doing comedy routines and magic tricks but did not dance. Instead, the Glamour Girls performed his choreography, dancing with huge feather fans to the song "That Old Black Magic" by the composers Harold Arlen and Johnny Mercer. This was the only time that Bob's father ever attended one of Bob's recitals.

High School Years

Bob was a shy boy in high school and never talked

Vaudeville at a Glance

Vaudeville was the most popular form of entertainment in the early 1900s. A vaudeville show combined many short acts of song, dance, and comedy. Dance routines had to be short and sweet, so performers would try to do everything in just a few minutes: go fast, go slow, be funny, do their favorite steps, and end with a big finish. Tricks like jumps, flips, and turns were sure to impress the crowd. Many famous vaudevillians had a signature step and were nicknamed for it, like Earl "Snakehips" Tucker. Several jazz steps were introduced by these vaudeville performers. For example, the Charleston, introduced by the Ziegfeld Follies in 1923, involved stepping forward and back, kicking one leg to the front, then the other to the back.

During the 1920s, young women who danced the Charleston were known as "flappers" because of the way their arms flapped while performing this popular social dance.

about his dancing. He continued to get good grades, competed in swimming and track, served as president of the senior class, and had a steady girlfriend. Not even his best friends knew he could dance until he agreed to appear in the school variety show his junior year. His friends were amazed and did not make fun of him like Bob thought they would. The following year, he and his two best friends dressed up as women to perform a routine. This practice is called performing in drag. Although it was just for fun, Bob always took his work seriously and rehearsed the boys constantly until everything was just right. When the three of them lip-synched to a song by the singing group the Andrews Sisters, their schoolmates went wild with applause.

By Bob's senior year, as the war was ending, the Riff Brothers were playing military shows in the area. This helped Bob decide that he would join the navy after graduation. But before that, he planned to take six months to try his hand at a professional career as a performer. He wanted his partner to come with him, but Charles was a year younger than he and decided to stay and finish high school. So Bob Fosse began performing solo as Bob Riff. The transition was not easy, however. Bob was too

Joseph Papp poses in 1983 in front of posters of his many successful productions. Born in Brooklyn, New York, he founded the New York Shakespeare Festival and the Public Theater.

old to be considered cute and too young to book major shows on his own. Soon, he was borrowing money from Weaver to last him until he went to boot camp.

Seaman Fosse

Once he became Seaman Fosse in 1945, Bob entered the entertainment branch of the navy based in New York City. For the next three months, he toured with one of five navy musicals performing for sailors overseas. Following this, he began working with a chief petty officer, or a top enlisted man in the navy, on a new show. The officer was Joseph Papirosky, who would later become the famous theatrical producer Joseph Papp. Bob became the star of their show, *Tough Situation*, which they performed throughout the South Pacific. In it, Bob performed solos, a comedy

13

routine, and a trio he also choreographed, which again involved performing in drag and lip-synching to the song "Boogie Woogie Bugle Boy," sung by the Andrews Sisters.

Bob's return from this tour marked the end of his navy duty. Most of the other young boys planned to return home to their families or sweethearts, but not Bob. He was moving to New York City where he and Joseph Papp would eventually meet again, not through the armed services, but through the theater. At age nineteen and with no official theatrical training, Bob Fosse was going to try his luck on Broadway.

2 Give a Guy a Break

A side from his early dance lessons and Riff Brothers rehearsals with Fred Weaver, Bob Fosse had no other formal dance training. This did not mean, however, that he ever stopped learning. Much of Bob's training happened on the job. The Riff Brothers often performed in showcases at several different types of venues, which meant that Bob and Charles were able to see many kinds of acts. They always paid attention to these performers, in addition to the movies that were sometimes shown before the live acts. These films often featured dancers such as Gene Kelly and Fred Astaire—men Bob Fosse would always try to emulate.

Many accomplished dancers, choreographers, or any other type of artists only succeed in professional careers after years of traditional study. Bob Fosse was different. Rather than take regular dance classes and seek out the master teachers in each form, he took charge of his own dance experiences. Every time Bob did a solo—as part of the Riff Brothers act, in his high school talent shows, or in a navy musical—he developed his skills as a choreographer because he created the performance himself. Many dancers like to perform steps made up by someone else, but Bob liked it better when he was in charge; he didn't want to move any way but his own.

Bob was also a very determined and hard worker. In preparing for a performance, he would rehearse his routines right up until curtain time. While in the midst of one project, he was always working on ideas for the future. He landed his first professional part after just two auditions in New York City—a national tour of *Call Me Mister*. He had a featured role as a dancer as well as some lines and singing. He was working with other great talents and visiting every major city in the country. He was incredibly grateful for such an opportunity and loved the experience, but was thinking ahead at the same time, to a future life in film instead of theater. A friend in the *Call Me Mister* company and others throughout Bob's life would recall this ambition as one of his strongest characteristics and perhaps the driving force of his career.

Bob Fosse and Janet Leigh perform a scene in *My Sister Eileen* (1955). Besides choreographing the movie, Bob played a character in love with the beautiful Eileen, who had moved to Manhattan with her brainy sister and had many admirers besides him.

Hollywood Calling

His first part in a Broadway show came just a few years later in *Dance Me a Song* (1950). It was not a great success, but it did give Bob a Broadway credit.

He was also beginning to get exposure with his dance partner and first wife, Mary-Ann Niles. They appeared as guest dancers on television and in variety show specials. Each little bit got him closer to his dream of dancing in the movies like Gene Kelly. He wouldn't have to wait long, either; *Give a Girl a Break* (1952) was Bob's big break into film. He bought a red convertible and moved to Hollywood to live the movie star life.

Give a Girl a Break had a great young cast that included Debbie Reynolds. Also, Bob got to work with one of the best directors in the business: Stanley Donen. In one dance scene, Bob was asked to do a backflip, something he had never done before. Bob preferred small, delicate movements and was scared to execute such a big acrobatic trick. But the one and only time he did it without support and in front of the camera,

it was perfect! No one ever knew he flew to New York and worked with a coach for two days to get it right.

Soon after this project, Bob landed a role in the film version of *Kiss Me, Kate* (1953) with Ann Miller. Although it was a small part, it would prove to be a wise career choice for Bob; he had asked for and was granted permission to choreograph a section of the song "From This Moment On." This scene quite possibly marks the birth of many trademarks of Bob Fosse's movement style. In it, Bob and dance partner, Carol Haney, snap their fingers, turn their knees and toes in, and take quick, tiny steps.

Bob Fosse, Tommy Rall, and Bobby Van woo Ann Miller in the song, "Tom, Dick, and Harry" in *Kiss Me, Kate* (1953). This was Fosse's smallest role on screen, but his style of choreography was born in the song "From This Moment On."

This duet would take the two dancers even further. Thanks to Joan McCracken, Bob's second wife, the famous Broadway producer George Abbot saw this on-screen performance. Joan was a Broadway veteran and favorite of Abbott's. So when she recommended her husband to choreograph Abbott's new musical, he trusted her. Bob then left his Hollywood dream behind to pursue the theater again.

It's Showtime, Folks!

Fosse on Film:

- *Give a Girl a Break*
- *The Affairs of Dobie Gillis*
- *Kiss Me, Kate*
- *My Sister Eileen*
- *Damn Yankees*
- *The Little Prince*
- *That's Entertainment, Part 2*
- *All That Jazz* (He does not appear in this, but it is based on his life.)

Steam Heat

The production team of *The Pajama Game* (1954) was nervous about hiring Bob. After all, his professional work as a choreographer amounted to only a few minutes in a single movie and certainly nothing in live theater beyond the Amundsen High School talent shows. But as it turned out, there was no need to worry. The discipline that Fred Weaver had instilled in Bob as a kid was now a natural part of the way Bob worked. With the help of George Abbott, Fosse figured out where each dance in the musical should be and how it was to fit into the story line.

The Pajama Game centered around pajama factory workers who wanted a pay raise. One scene that needed a dance number was a union meeting that offered a bit of

"Steam Heat" is danced by Eddie Phillips, Carol Haney, and Buzz Miller in the movie version of *The Pajama Game* (1957). Fosse's precise movements took many hours of rehearsal to master.

light entertainment provided by the workers themselves, almost like the talent and variety shows Bob knew so well. Songwriters Richard Adler and Jerry Ross had written a simple tune based on sound effects called "Steam Heat."

Still a hoofer at heart, Fosse loved creating movement to the percussive, rhythmic elements of the song. By the time rehearsals began, Bob had worked out the entire dance in his head. His pal Carol Haney, along with dancers Buzz Miller and Peter Gennaro, learned it in no time.

Wearing black suits, derby hats, and white gloves, the trio punctuated the bells and whistles by tipping their hats, rolling their shoulders, and chugging across the stage. On opening night, the number stopped the show. To this day, "Steam Heat," Fosse's first piece of choreography for Broadway, remains one of the most famous in musical theater history.

3 The Fosse Signature Style

From that moment on, Bob Fosse would never have to worry about a job again. After one more try at a movie career with a film called *My Sister Eileen* (1955), Bob went right back to Broadway to choreograph a new musical being developed about baseball. *Damn Yankees* (1955) tells the story of Joe, an aging man who sells his soul to the devil for a chance to be a young baseball hero. Working to help the devil's plan along is the beautiful and irresistible Lola.

At this time Bob met Gwen Verdon. Gwen had been dancing since childhood, first studying with her mother, then with Jack Cole, who had trained with modern dance pioneers Ruth St. Denis and Ted Shawn. Before meeting Gwen, Bob was not sure that he and Gwen would get along, perhaps because their performance backgrounds were so different. But when Bob gave Gwen a few steps to try out, it was as if she had been born to dance like Bob.

Damn Yankees was popular; however, it was not the hit everyone expected it to be on Broadway. Still, it was successful for Bob and Gwen. The show made Gwen Verdon a star and gave Bob not only a second Broadway credit, but a dancer talented enough to perform his movement style. Most important, however, it brought Gwen and Bob together, and they fell in love with each other.

Bob the Choreographer

While Gwen played Lola eight times a week at the 46th St. Theatre, Bob returned to Los Angeles to make the movie version of *The Pajama Game*. This time, he choreographed alongside his friend and director Stanley Donen. While shooting the dance scenes, especially "Once a Year Day," which took place in a park, Bob paid close attention and learned a lot from Donen about camera angles, lenses, and other directing concerns.

Bob went back to New York to choreograph the show *Bells Are Ringing* (1955), but quickly returned to Los Angeles, this time with Gwen, to make the film version of *Damn Yankees*. Again, Stanley Donen was directing, Bob was choreographing, and Gwen, of course, was starring as Lola.

There is a scene in *Damn Yankees* that is very similar to the "Steam Heat" scene in *The Pajama Game*: two baseball fans (one is Lola in disguise) perform a dance for Joe and the others at a team event. "Who's Got the Pain?" is short and catchy, a little mambo with few lyrics and lots of "ughs!" and "erps!" In the movie, Bob himself performs this duet with Gwen.

Even though he came to realize that he was much better at working behind the scenes, Bob would always yearn to perform

Gwen Verdon and Bob Fosse perform "Who's Got the Pain?" in the movie version of *Damn Yankees* (1958). Before shooting the scene, Bob had insisted that the couple be closely watched to make sure they were exactly together in their movements. The result was a documented flawless performance.

Be Like Bob

Signature Fosse Costume Pieces:

- Black pants or leotard
- Black shoes
- Bowler hat
- White gloves
- White socks
- Cane

Signature Fosse Moves:

Puppy Dog Hands: dancer bends his or her elbows and puts arms in front of himself/herself, breaking his or her wrists so hands hang down, like a puppy begging

Strut: dancer sticks his or her pelvis out, leans way back, and takes long, stretchy strides leading with his or her feet

Hat Trick: dancer flips hat off his or her head from behind and catches it in front of his or her waist

again and this was the perfect chance. He and Gwen have a playful chemistry on-screen and make the movements look very easy. They strut with their pelvises pushed forward, lean against each other's backs and scoot out until their torsos are parallel to the floor, and accentuate all the nonsense syllables with shoulder rolls, hip rolls, and even eye rolls. Many dancers over time have become quite good at performing in the Fosse style, but this scene might be its truest representation. Who better to perform Fosse's technique than Bob and the one dancer who helped make it so famous?

The Couple in Demand

Soon, Broadway producers were racing to work with the successful couple. After filming was over, they were asked to be part of a musical called *New Girl in Town* (1957), of course as choreographer and leading lady. Then came *Redhead* (1959). Gwen agreed to play the lead in this new musical under one condition—Bob would be the director.

Bob put himself under enormous pressure in this new role. This was his first directing job, and he was also choreographing the dances. He worked harder than he ever worked before, which also meant that he was very hard on the dancers and actors. The work was also stressful for Gwen. She was so much the star that the show was named for her (her red hair always made her stand out). Plus, the amount of singing and dancing she had to do was more than she usually did.

However, all their hard work paid off. Audiences and critics loved *Redhead*. One Fosse convention that was proving quite successful was his use of vaudeville. Although *Redhead* was set in London in the early 1900s, the music hall scenes were performed by dancers with bowler hats and canes doing standard vaudeville movements mixed with Fosse's turned-in knees and sideways shuffling.

Starting a Family

Bob had divorced Joan McCracken years earlier. He and Gwen married in 1960 and planned to start a family. The possibility of pregnancy meant that Gwen had to retire from the theater for a time.

When Gwen became pregnant, Bob was left to work on his own. He co-directed *Little Me* (1962) with his good friend Cy Feuer. By this time, Bob had become very creative with large group numbers. "The Rich Kids' Rag" in *Little Me* stands out for

this reason. Dressed in black, with the usual white gloves and socks that Fosse favored, the dancers pranced around with their noses in the air. Through simple movements like this, Fosse was able to make a funny dance mocking the behaviors of snooty rich kids.

Nicole Providence Fosse was born on March 24, 1963. Like her parents, she would grow up to be an entertainer. She would later perform in *Phantom of the Opera* and offer assistance with *Fosse*, a show created after her father's death.

Sweet Charity

In 1965, Bob began writing a script himself, based

Gwen Verdon, Bob Fosse, and Nicole Fosse celebrate the opening of Fosse's show *Dancin'* on March 27, 1978. Even after separating in the early 1970s, Bob Fosse and Verdon always remained very close. He considered Nicole, his only child who also had a career as a performer, the darling of his life.

on a book called *Nights of Cabiria*. Bob found it very difficult and asked his friend, the popular playwright Neil Simon, to help him out. Not only did Simon help, but he took over. Between Fosse and Simon, *Sweet Charity* (1966) was born.

Sweet Charity appeals to audiences on many levels. It is full of upbeat songs and high energy dancing. Each number, from "Hey, Big Spender" to "The Rich Man's Frug," can be watched by itself and enjoyed every time. The story and characters are also rich in color. Charity Hope Valentine was a young dance hall hostess with a string of bad boyfriends and dreams of getting a better job and falling in love. Between Bob Fosse, Neil Simon, and songwriters Cy Coleman and Dorothy Fields, *Sweet Charity* was sure to be a powerful piece of musical theater.

Added to that was the much-anticipated return of Gwen Verdon to the stage. After a five-year absence, she would be coming out of retirement to play Charity. It could be said that she worked harder on this show than her husband. Besides being the star and performing many musical numbers, such as "If My Friends Could See Me Now," she also served as Bob's dance assistant since her character was not in most of the ensemble numbers.

Like *Redhead*, Gwen provided much of the inspiration for developing the lead character in *Sweet Charity*. For that reason, it seemed quite possible that this musical could end when she stopped playing it, like *Redhead* had. But *Sweet Charity* did not only sustain a long run on Broadway, it also toured the country and was even revived in 1986. Other actresses who would get

Fosse rehearses Shirley MacLaine on the movie set of *Sweet Charity* (1969). Fosse wanted movement to work as a character study rather than mere dance steps.

to play Charity Hope Valentine included Ann Reinking and Debbie Allen. Shirley MacLaine, another redhead, had the honor of re-creating the role for film in 1968.

Fosse the Director

Sweet Charity was Bob Fosse's first film directing job, and he found that he loved it. In fact, he would go on to make a handful of movies in his life that were not based on previous Broadway shows. Some, like *Lenny* and *Star 80*, had nothing to do with dance at all.

Many people believe that *Cabaret* was Bob's best film. In terms of sheer recognition, this certainly holds true. It starred a young actress named Liza Minnelli, who played Sally Bowles, an American nightclub performer who lived and worked in Germany just before Adolf Hitler rose to power. *Cabaret* had been a stage show first, but did not involve Fosse. In fact, he turned it down because he didn't think it could work. But film was another story. Besides casting Joel Grey as the Master of Ceremonies, not much of the movie remained anything like the stage version. Supporting characters were cut, and new ones added. The same happened with songs.

Fosse's goal was to make sure that every song used in the production fit realistically into the plot and even helped to move the story along. This meant that instead of characters suddenly breaking into song on the street corner or in an office, singing took place where it was meant to be—in this case, on the stage of the Kit Kat Klub. Therefore, only the actors whose characters were performers in the cabaret got to sing and dance in the film. The cabaret, then, functioned as a musical narration of the stories happening in the characters' lives. For instance, after Sally gets excited because the man she met at the cleaners turns out to be very rich, she is onstage with the Master of Ceremonies singing, "Money makes the world go around."

Fosse's choreography does many jobs in *Cabaret*. It comments on the action happening before and after the dance scenes, it offers light-hearted entertainment and comic relief, and it helps to create a sense of the historical time. Fosse was careful to include the dark humor and risqué behavior common to German cabaret performers of the 1930s. His own background in vaudeville and music halls made it easy for him to relate to these sensibilities. In most projects after *Cabaret*, he would continue to explore this dark and risqué behavior in his choreographic style.

A Very Big Year

Cabaret was released in 1972, one of the biggest years of Bob Fosse's life. In October of that year, *Pippin* opened on Broadway at the Imperial Theatre. This musical told the story of a prince in the Holy Roman Empire and starred John Rubinstein as the prince and Ben Vereen as the Leading Player. Ann Reinking started her legendary career with Fosse here in the ensemble. In the same year, the creative team of *Cabaret*, Fosse and songwriters John Kander and Fred Ebb, collaborated on *Liza with a Z*, a musical show for the rising star, Liza Minnelli. The show, which was created for stage and also filmed as a concert for television, was strictly song and dance. It included dances to popular songs like "Bye Bye, Blackbird" and "God Bless the Child." With these three shows, Bob Fosse would become the only person to win a

Liza Minelli as Sally Bowles and Joel Grey as the Master of Ceremonies perform "Money Makes the World Go Around" at the Kit Kat Klub in the movie *Cabaret* (1972). Fosse tried to re-create the actual style of dance and performance in pre-World War II German cabarets for all the dance numbers in the film.

Tony, Emmy, and Academy Award all in the same year.

In 1975, it was time for Gwen Verdon to make another comeback, this time with *Chicago*. The original version of this musical was quite different from the 1996 revival and nothing like the 2002 movie. Tony Stevens was Bob's assistant for *Chicago* and, in an interview with the author of this book, remembers the choreographer setting several goals for himself while making the show. First, he said to Stevens, "Don't let me do anything I've already done." Never being able to escape his vaudeville roots, Fosse also wanted to base each number in *Chicago* on a different real-life entertainer. *Chicago* was a story straight out of the Charleston era, but Stevens remembers Fosse denying himself the use of that famous step. Stevens describes the movement and costumes as having a circus influence with lots of neon colors—very much the opposite of the sleek black look in Ann

Reinking's version twenty years later.

During rehearsals for *Chicago*, Bob, a chain-smoker since childhood, started experiencing chest pains. He was diagnosed with a heart condition and had to have bypass surgery. The show was suspended during Bob's hospital stay and recuperation. Rehearsals did resume and *Chicago*, starring Gwen Verdon and Chita Rivera, did quite well on Broadway. However, it was overshadowed by the amazing success of *A Chorus Line*, produced by Joseph Papp, Fosse's navy friend, that same year.

4 All That Jazz

Once the show *Chicago* was up and running, Fosse turned his attention to a new, original movie inspired by his recent near-death experience in the hospital. *All That Jazz* is technically a work of fiction but bears a striking resemblance to Bob's own life. The main character, Joe Gideon, is developing a new Broadway musical and editing a movie at the same time. He is separated from his dancer wife, but they are still good friends and able to work together on the show (also true of Bob and Gwen). Joe has a young daughter aspiring to be a dancer (like Nicole) and several dancer girlfriends who fuel his work as a choreographer (also true and common knowledge among Bob's peers).

Joe overworks himself and lands in the hospital where he confronts his fear of dying. Similar to *Cabaret*, where the songs in the Kit Kat Klub added to the story, dance numbers in *All That Jazz* come from rehearsal scenes for the new musical. However, Fosse finds additional ways to make them work and serve an overall purpose in the film. In one scene, Joe's daughter, Michelle, and girlfriend (played by Ann Reinking on- and off-screen) perform for fun in his living room. Once in the hospital, Joe has dream sequences in the form of song and dance about what it would be like

Roy Scheider as Joe Gideon on his deathbed surrounded by dancers in a dream sequence in *All That Jazz*. This number, with the dancers holding huge feather fans, was a convention Fosse used in "Razzle-Dazzle" in *Chicago*, as well as in *Dancin'* and *New Girl in Town*.

if he died. With all these similarities between the real and the make-believe, it is also safe to bet that Joe Gideon's paranoia, perfectionism, and seriousness were reflections of Bob's own character. Indeed, *All That Jazz* was a very honest portrayal of Bob's less-than-perfect life.

Discipline is Freedom

As Tony Stevens puts it, "Being able to recognize your limitations and make them work for you is what makes someone a star. Bob Fosse was certainly a star." Stevens was Fosse's assistant on the original production of *Chicago* and recalls the beauty of the movement he learned

there. Bob broke movement down to the smallest of gestures. "Every single move meant something," Stevens explains, "and there was nothing in there that didn't need to be."

This minimalism was probably the key to Fosse's dances. No one was better at saying so much with so little. Rather than a dancer coordinating several movements at once, Bob would ask for a different kind of coordination from his dancers: the ability to move one part of the body at a time, a practice called isolation. When a dancer's entire body is completely still and only his or her fingers are drumming on the front of the hip—the action appears as big as a triple pirouette.

Looking back at all of Bob Fosse's work, it is easy to pick out the moves he especially loved and the traits that made his choreography unique. When Bob was young, his teacher would scold him for turning his knees and feet in instead of out. This would later become his favorite move. As seen in "Steam Heat," Fosse also loved noises. If the dancers were not making noise themselves, by snapping, clapping, or stomping, they were accenting sounds in the music with looks, kicks, drags, or a simple fan of the fingers.

Part of his originality lay in what he did not include. Most other choreographers working at the same time based their movements on ballet technique. Bob never learned ballet steps such as grand jetés and arabesques, so it made sense that he did not think to include them. He preferred to tell stories with gestures even non-dancers could understand, like a funny walk or a tilt of the head.

Stevens remembers a time when the cast of *Chicago* rehearsed the wiggling of one finger for four hours. "It was hard to rehearse so rigorously and so specifically, but in the end, when you saw the beautiful effect it created, it was always worth it." One important lesson Stevens learned from his experience with

And the Award Goes to . . . Bob Fosse

In 1973, Bob Fosse became the only person to earn the triple crown of entertainment awards: an Emmy (for *Liza with a Z*), a Tony (for *Pippin*), and an Oscar (for *Cabaret*).

His first two jobs on Broadway, *The Pajama Game* and *Damn Yankees*, won him Tony Awards for best choreography.

All in all, Bob Fosse received one Oscar, three Emmys, and ten Tonys for his work as a choreographer, director, and producer.

After his death, he was honored with an American Choreography Heritage Award (given by the American Choreography Award organization). The revival of *Chicago*, choreographed by Ann Reinking in Fosse's style, won a Tony and a Laurence Olivier Theatre Award.

Fosse was that "discipline is freedom."

His Legacy Lives On

After *All That Jazz*, Fosse created two other original shows: a musical revue called *Dancin'* in 1978 and the original musical *Big Deal* in 1986. Then, on September 23, 1987, Bob and Gwen were rehearsing a touring company of *Sweet Charity* in Washington, D.C. On their way to the hotel to get ready for the evening's performance, Bob Fosse collapsed on the sidewalk and died of heart failure. Family, friends, and dancers mourned the loss of a beloved person and artist.

However, his work lives on. Even in 1999, twelve years after his death, Fosse was still making it big on Broadway—literally. A new production called *Fosse* opened on January 14, and played for two and a half years before traveling around the world. The show was conceived and staged by Ann Reinking. Gwen Verdon served as an artistic adviser before her death in 2000. *Fosse* starred several dancers who devoted much of their careers to working with the choreographer. Reinking, Ben Vereen, and Bebe Neuwirth, who first worked with Fosse in *Dancin'* in 1982, all took their turns leading the cast. Fosse also offered a chance for a younger generation of dancers to experience a lot of the work of this famous choreographer all at once.

With pieces from *The Pajama Game*, *Sweet Charity*, and *Dancin'* all rolled into one show, it is easy to pick out traits of Bob's style and his movement preferences. Not only are the musicals of Bob Fosse lasting artifacts of his contributions to the world of dance, his style itself is considered to be its own vocabulary. In other words, general jazz or ballet

Dancers strike a classic Fosse pose in *Fosse*, the musical retrospective of one of Broadway's most powerful influences. *Fosse* won the Tony Award for best musical in 1999. This photo is of a performance in London, England, at the Prince of Wales Theatre.

dance training, while incredibly important, will not fully prepare a dancer to properly execute Fosse's choreography. As discussed in earlier chapters, Fosse incorporated many moves that did not come from any form of technique already established. He "turned in" when everyone else "turned out." He asked his dancers to "flex" when they had

Fosse rehearses dancers in 1965. Many dancers who worked with him felt he made them exceed their own expectations of how well they could dance.

he was self-conscious of his own thinning hair and wore gloves because he didn't like his hands.

A Living Tradition

Elements of Fosse's style are being taught all the time. Many dancers who were able to work with him are also teachers and travel around the world giving workshops. Some, like Tony Stevens, have become choreographers themselves and find that their own work is influenced by what they learned from Fosse.

been taught for several years to "point."

Fosse liked to make these moves look even more striking by dressing the dancer in a black costume and white gloves. He also made wide use of props, especially bowler hats. Many say that he liked using hats because

Using a system called labanotation, much of Bob Fosse's choreography has been written down. Just as a musician can read a composition and learn it from paper, a dancer who knows how to read labanotation can learn a dance made by someone else. Dance is a living art form. Unlike a sculpture or painting that can stay around forever, dance is gone as soon as it appears. Re-creating important works of dance becomes harder and harder as time goes by. Besides videos, DVDs, and the physical act of passing choreography from one dancer to another, labanotation is a way of preserving dance for future generations. Using these tools together, it is possible to learn a piece of Bob Fosse's choreography today, even though he himself is no longer here to teach it.

Dance is a living tradition, and Bob Fosse will always play an important part in it. His work, like any other, is really only preserved and passed on through the human body. Through generations of dancers, his work lives on, inspiring and entertaining audiences worldwide with beauty, magic, and all that jazz.

Glossary

accentuate To emphasize or single out as important.

arabesque A basic ballet position where the body is supported on one leg, while the other leg extends behind the body. The arms form a position to create the longest possible line from fingertips to the toes that extend behind the dancer's body.

cabaret A nightclub with musical entertainment.

Charleston era A period in American history (the 1920s) in which the Charleston was a popular dance and signified the carefree attitude of society.

convention A custom; usual practice or habit that is widely accepted.

emulate To imitate in an effort to strive to be equal.

execute To carry out or to perform an action.

grand jeté A long jump starting from one leg and landing on the other. The dancer appears to be doing the splits in midair.

hoofer A name used to refer to a rhythm tap dancer, or a professional musical theater dancer.

minimalism A style in art in which only the simplest designs and forms are used, often in repetition.

percussive Striking one thing against another to make noise musically.

perfectionism The act of always striving to be perfect, and anything short of this being unacceptable.

revival A new production of a show that has already been produced in the past.

venue A place where a performance occurs.

For More Information

Internet Broadway Database
League of American Theatres & Producers
226 West 47 Street
New York, NY 10036
Web site: www.ibdb.com

Jazz Dance World Congress
International Headquarters
614 Davis Street
Evanston, IL 60201
(847) 475-1432
Web site: www.jazzdanceworldcongress.org

National Museum of Dance & Hall of Fame
99 South Broadway
Saratoga Springs, NY 12866-9809
(518) 584-2225
Web site: www.dancemuseum.org

Web Sites

Due to the changing nature of Internet links, the Rosen Publishing Group, Inc., has developed an on-line list of Web sites related to the subject of this book. This site is updated regularly. Please use this link to access the list:

http://www.rosenlinks.com/lac/bofo

For Further Reading

Alter, Judy. *Vaudeville: The Birth of Show Business*. Danbury, CT: Franklin Watts, 1998.

Cutcher, Jenai. *Gotta Dance: The Rhythms of Jazz and Tap*. New York, NY: Rosen Publishing Group, 2004.

Kraines, Minda Goodman, and Esther Pryor. *Jump into Jazz: The Basics and Beyond for Jazz Dance Students*. New York, NY: McGraw-Hill, 2000.

Long, Robert Emmet. *Broadway, the Golden Years: Jerome Robbins and the Great Choreographer Directors, 1940 to the Present*. New York, NY: Continuum International Publishing Group, 2003.

Bibliography

Cutcher, Jenai. Interview with Tony Stevens, August 17, 2004.

Ebb, Fred, and John Kander, with Greg Lawrence. *Colored Lights: Forty Years of Words and Music, Show Biz, Collaboration, and All That Jazz*. New York, NY: Faber & Faber, 2003.

Gottfried, Martin. *All His Jazz: The Life and Death of Bob Fosse*. New York, NY: Da Capo Press, 2003.

Stearns, Marshall Winslow. *Jazz Dance: The Story of American Vernacular Dance*. New York, NY: Da Capo Press, 1994.

Index

About the Author

Jenai Cutcher dances, teaches, and writes, among other things. Born in Ohio, she now lives in New York City.

Photo Credits

Cover © Time Life Pictures/Getty Images; cover (background), pp. 1, 11, 42 © Bettmann/Corbis; pp. 6, 30 © John Springer Collection/Corbis; p. 13 © Jacques M. Chenet/Corbis; pp. 17, 19, 21, 24, 33, 36 © Everett Collection; p. 28 © AP/World Photos; p. 41 © Robbie Jack/Corbis.

Designer: Tahara Anderson; Editor: Leigh Ann Cobb
Developmental Editor: Nancy Allison, CMA, RME